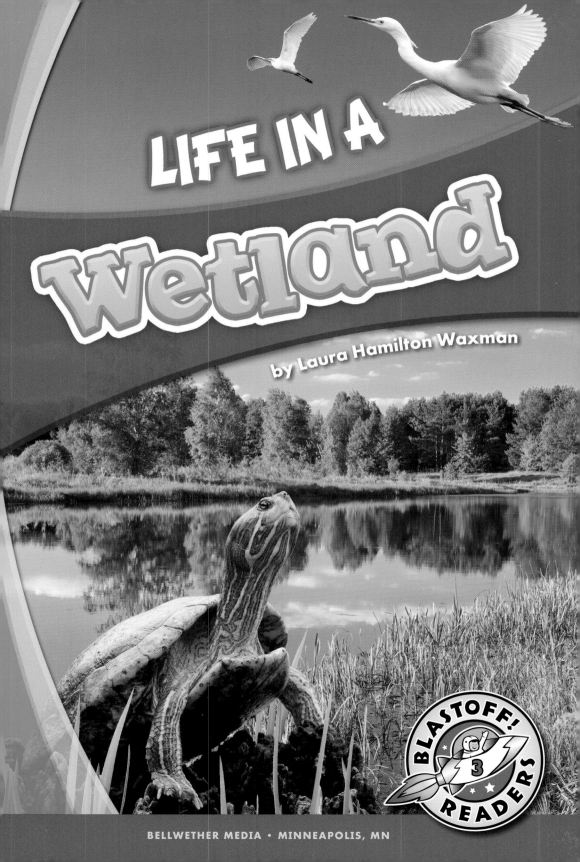

LIFE IN A
Wetland

by Laura Hamilton Waxman

BELLWETHER MEDIA • MINNEAPOLIS, MN

Note to Librarians, Teachers, and Parents:

Blastoff! Readers are carefully developed by literacy experts and combine standards-based content with developmentally appropriate text.

Level 1 provides the most support through repetition of high-frequency words, light text, predictable sentence patterns, and strong visual support.

Level 2 offers early readers a bit more challenge through varied simple sentences, increased text load, and less repetition of high-frequency words.

Level 3 advances early-fluent readers toward fluency through increased text and concept load, less reliance on visuals, longer sentences, and more literary language.

Level 4 builds reading stamina by providing more text per page, increased use of punctuation, greater variation in sentence patterns, and increasingly challenging vocabulary.

Level 5 encourages children to move from "learning to read" to "reading to learn" by providing even more text, varied writing styles, and less familiar topics.

Whichever book is right for your reader, Blastoff! Readers are the perfect books to build confidence and encourage a love of reading that will last a lifetime!

This edition first published in 2016 by Bellwether Media, Inc.

No part of this publication may be reproduced in whole or in part without written permission of the publisher. For information regarding permission, write to Bellwether Media, Inc., Attention: Permissions Department, 5357 Penn Avenue South, Minneapolis, MN 55419.

Library of Congress Cataloging-in-Publication Data

Waxman, Laura Hamilton, author.
 Life in a Wetland / by Laura Hamilton Waxman.
    pages cm. – (Blastoff! Readers. Biomes Alive!)
 Summary: "Simple text and full-color photography introduce beginning readers to life in a wetland. Developed by literacy experts for students in kindergarten through third grade"– Provided by publisher.
 Audience: Ages 5-8.
 Audience: K to grade 3.
 Includes bibliographical references and index.
 ISBN 978-1-62617-322-4 (hardcover : alk. paper)
 1. Wetland ecology–Juvenile literature. 2. Wetland animals–Juvenile literature. 3. Wetlands–Climatic factors–Juvenile literature. I. Title.
 QH541.5.M3W3355 2016
 577.68–dc23
                              2015035556

Printed in the United States of America, North Mankato, MN.

Table of Contents

The Wetland Biome

Brazos Bend
State Park,
Texas

Wetlands are a soggy **biome**.
These lands hold water or soak it
up like a sponge!

Earth needs these places to stay healthy. Wetlands keep water clean and stop floods. They also provide homes and food for many living things.

great egret

Three main types of wetlands are found around the world. They are **marshes**, **swamps**, and **bogs**.

marsh

swamp

bog

Most wetlands lie at the edges of lakes, rivers, or oceans. Wetlands near seas are filled with salt water. Those by rivers or lakes hold **freshwater**.

equator

wetlands =

N
W   E
S

The Climate

Amazon basin, Brazil

A wetland's distance from the **equator** determines its **climate**. Those in the **tropics** stay warm all year.

Wetlands far north are cold most of the time. **Temperate** wetlands often have warm summers and cool winters.

Placer River Valley, Alaska

Wetlands may hold water all year long or have wet and dry periods. Some **freeze** in winter.

Many wetlands
get a lot of rain in
spring. Others get
little rain and can
completely dry out!

The Plants

bald cypress trees

Wetland plants have **adapted** to live in water. The trees that fill swamps are often wide at the bottom. This helps them stay in place.

Many mangrove trees grow
roots aboveground. These
roots carry needed air to roots
under water.

roots

mangrove trees

Grasses and floating
plants fill the world's
marshes. Their long
stems and roots
hold them down in
watery soil.

cattails

water lilies

Lahemaa National Park, Estonia

moss

peat

Moss covers bogs and becomes **peat**. The peat is brown like soil and made of rotting moss.

great blue
heron

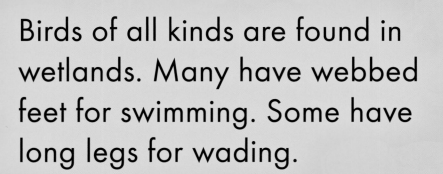
mallard
duck

Birds of all kinds are found in wetlands. Many have webbed feet for swimming. Some have long legs for wading.

16

Birds pluck plants and insects from the wet soil with their beaks. Some must watch out for hungry **reptiles**.

American alligator

European
common frog
tadpole

Amphibians are built to live in wetlands. They are born in water with bodies like fish.

Over time, they grow legs and feet. Then they crawl onto land to begin a new life!

froglet

adult

The Everglades

Location: Florida, United States

Size: 4,300 square miles (11,100 square kilometers)

Temperature:

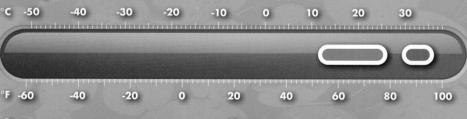

- **Dry season temperatures: 54 °F to 77 °F (12 °C to 25 °C)**
- **Wet season temperatures: 86 °F to 95 °F (30 °C to 35 °C)**

Precipitation: 60 inches (152 centimeters) per year

EVERGLADES FOOD WEB

American alligator

apple snail

great blue heron

southern leopard frog

saw grass

dragonfly

Other important plants: **mangrove trees, turtle grass, swamp lilies, mint, orchids, gumbo-limbo trees**

Other important animals: **crocodiles, ospreys, bald eagles, Florida panthers, salamanders**

Glossary

adapted—changed to survive in new conditions

amphibians—animals that live both on land and in water

biome—a nature community defined by its climate, land features, and living things

bogs—wetlands filled with spongy peat

climate—the specific weather conditions for an area

equator—the imaginary line that divides Earth into northern and southern halves

freeze—to turn from water into ice; water freezes at 32 degrees Fahrenheit (0 degrees Celsius).

freshwater—water that is not salty

marshes—wetlands filled with grasses and other plants with stems

peat—partly decayed plants that are spongy and brown

reptiles—cold-blooded animals that have backbones and lay eggs

roots—the parts of a plant that keep it in place and take in water

swamps—wetlands filled with trees and other woody plants

temperate—mild; not too hot or too cold.

tropics—a hot region near the equator

To Learn More

AT THE LIBRARY

Heos, Bridget. *Do You Really Want to Visit a Wetland?* Mankato, Minn.: Amicus Illustrated, 2015.

Newland, Sonya. *Wetland Animals*. Mankato, Minn.: Smart Apple Media, 2012.

Silverman, Buffy. *Wetlands*. Chicago, Ill.: Raintree, 2013.

ON THE WEB

Learning more about wetlands is as easy as 1, 2, 3.

1. Go to www.factsurfer.com.

2. Enter "wetlands" into the search box.

3. Click the "Surf" button and you will see a list of related web sites.

With factsurfer.com, finding more information is just a click away.

Index